Salvaging the Sacred:

My Sister Lucy

by

Marian Partington

Quaker Books

2004

Acknowledgements

With deep gratitude to: Ch'an Buddhist teachers, Dr. John Crook and Master Sheng-yen for the healing refuge of silent retreats and the transmission of Buddhist wisdom. Deborah Orr (journalist and editor of the Guardian Weekend in 1996) who delivered this essay into the public domain with sensitivity and integrity. Marion McNaughton and other trustees of the Joseph Rowntree Charitable Trust, and my 'support group' (Alison Leonard, Iris Tute and Jan Caine) who upheld this journey. Woodbrooke Tutor Pam Lunn whose skilful interview at the Summer Gathering brought this work into a wider Quaker community. Tim Newell who invited me to contribute to his project Restorative Justice in Prisons. Marian Liebmann, Barbara Tudor and Lindy Wootton who have worked with me in Bristol Prison, and Mark Fernley who found his inner light and dared to change. The many friends and fellow-travellers whose prayerful support helps me to trust what arises. My dear partner Nick Salt and our children (Aaron, Luke , Marigold and Jack). My mother, father, brothers and their families. Finally, thank you Lucy, your life and death have deepened my knowledge of love. I will try to pass that on.

*

The text of this pamphlet was first published in a slightly different version in the *Guardian Weekend*, 18th May 1996 and reprinted in the *Guardian Year Book* 1996. This edition January 2004 by Quaker Books.

Salvaging the Sacred

L UCY PARTINGTON was my sister, four years younger than me. On 27th December 1973 she left a friend's house in time to walk to the bus stop in Evesham Road, Cheltenham, intending to catch the 10.15pm bus back to our home in Gretton. She didn't catch the bus. She was twenty one years old and in her final year of an English degree at Exeter University. She was reported missing and a national search was launched. She became one of thousands of "missing people" for twenty years.

On 4th March 1994—her birthday—Frederick West told the Investigation Team in Gloucester that there were more bodies in the basement of 25 Cromwell St, and that one of them was Lucy's. The details about the criminals and the crime have been on general release in the media for several months at a time over the past two years. They warranted a "V chip" or at least an 18 certificate. Or will the "V chip" only apply to fiction?

The grotesque details surrounding Lucy's death are part of my life. I can't pretend it didn't happen. I work hard to understand. I remind myself that Lucy went through it only once and that we can never know exactly what happened. But there is something about trying to get the measure of it before I can let go of it. It is vast and slippery. It is sticky and staining.

Most of Lucy's bones, her poetry and her soul, have survived. We will never know how she coped with what must be one of the worst possible ways to die. But let us not forget that many women, children and men are violently abused and killed in war, domestic violence and random murder every day.

There are many theories about the short term and long term effects of trauma, and many of them are pessimistic. Yet the Chinese word for "crisis" has two meanings: "danger" and "opportunity for change". I feel it is time to speak about my way through all this. I have been given a valuable chance to deepen my powers of compassion by facing the reality of my deepest fears. I am offering my attempt to find words and images to describe significant moments in my grapplings as I struggle to come to terms with what is essentially beyond reason and in many ways beyond words.

But words must be found. There must be something for all of us to learn from this profoundly shocking profanity before it gets buried under the concrete of fear, prejudice, or even worse, indifference. I am offering you where I have got to so far in all this. It is speaking about Lucy's truth, in her life and in her death. It is about poetry and transformation. It is about my quest to find meaning by trying to remain open to the pain, the joy, the rage, the grief, and what lies beyond. It is about living with the reality of violence, rape, torture and murder, trying to face up to it and trying to transform it. It is not always rational. I have followed my heart. It is a rite of passage. It is purgatorial. It is about time. It is about salvaging the sacred.

When I say, "My sister was murdered, she was one of the Wests' victims," it makes my throat ache. It was easier to say "My sister disappeared," but more difficult to live with that sense of unresolved loss.

Lucy was lucky to come from a family who loved her. We are led to believe that the majority of the young women in this case were not so fortunate. "They" managed to get lost without many people noticing or searching. "They" did not have much of a sense of purpose or direction in their lives. "They" have been labelled as "natural victims". If someone chooses to hitch-hike, does that mean that she is more deserving of a terrible end to her life than someone like Lucy, who had strong opinions about not hitch-hiking? Every one of the girls and young women in "the West Case" had a right to live. Heather,

Charmaine, Lynda, Juanita, Therese, Shirley, Carol, Alison, Shirley Ann, Rena, Anne and the two unborn babies. Their lives had equal value. It seems important to remember this.

When Lucy "disappeared", the dilemma caused by the huge sense of loss with no opportunity to grieve properly didn't fade as the years went by. On an emotional level I hardly dared to imagine that she had been murdered, and sometimes I hoped that she was still alive. For a while I wondered if she had gone off to join a nunnery ... or committed suicide. One of the most painful aspects of her disappearance was the feeling that we had never paid tribute, as a family, to her life. The subject almost became taboo. Part of me was stuck in the past. Part of me was terrified of us all dying and never knowing what had happened to her; no chance to honour her life. Eventually, twenty years after her disappearance, most of our family gathered together to plant a special tree in memory of Lucy.

This is how my daughter Marigold described it in 1994, when she was sixteen:

"Although it seemed like a good idea to put Lucy to rest, the atmosphere felt really uncomfortable. Something wasn't quite right, because everyone found it really difficult to talk about her. This made me realise how painful the situation was and how devastating it was for them not knowing what had happened to her, and perhaps, never knowing."

It is very difficult to find the words or an image to describe the pain and disorientation of one's sister simply disappearing without trace, for twenty years. It's a bit like trying to search for a body that is trapped somewhere beneath the frozen Arctic ocean, as the freeze continues and the ice thickens and there is no sign of a thaw, no sign of a seal hole. The features of that world become distorted as the seasons pass and the ice builds up, and you have to go inside to get warm if you want to survive and carry on. But you have to be ready for the thaw, for the rescue. Somewhere inside I became disconnected from the past and disabled by the future.

However, two months after our tree-planting ceremony we began to find out what had happened to her. I kept a diary at that time. Here are a few jottings. The only words that came to me at that time are mostly brief and factual, the result of a state of shock and a certain amount of denial.

*

Tuesday 1st March 1994
Phone call from Mum warning me that the Press are suggesting that the third unidentified body that has been dug up in the garden of 25 Cromwell Street might be Lucy. They have been hassling her about it. The police haven't been in touch.

Wednesday 2nd March
Came across a paper at work and read about the three bodies. Date of unidentified body. Female in late twenties. That evening phoned Mum and said I felt we should contact the police.

Thursday 3rd March
Contacted the police in Gloucester. They said that they were following a line of inquiry and that they were almost certain that it was not Lucy. Because it's Lucy's birthday tomorrow and because the press speculation and horror of it all is stirring up our pain and anxiety I decide to go and spend the day with Mum.

Friday 4th March
Lucy's birthday. Radio news before I set off has put the dates back on the third body (now died any time after 1972, body in early twenties). Mention that West lived in Bishop's Cleeve, which is on the bus route to Gretton from Cheltenham, is making me sure that this must be to do with Lucy. Spent the day keeping busy but feeling a terrible sense of unease and dread.

Saturday 5th March

10.15am phone call from the police saying that they would like to come over to talk to us. They have some "news" for us. That half hour of waiting for them to arrive was full of a terrible restlessness and anxiety ... palpitations and nausea. The numbness and muteness of shock began to invade. Two youngish plain-clothes policeman arrived. They introduce themselves as Brian Smith ("Smudger") and Russell Williams. I notice Brian's polished brown shoes and his red tie and the scar on Russell's face. There is a pause. Then Russell confirms our worst fears. Fred West has been talking to the police and has told them that there are more bodies in the basement and that one of them is called Lucy. They have begun to dig. It was a lovely sunny afternoon and I felt like going for a walk up Gretton Hill. However, we went shopping in Cheltenham. Denial was setting in. Numerous messages on the answering machine on our return. The Pain Vultures sounding as if it's unquestionable that we should call them back (TV and tabloids). We don't. By now they know that three more bodies have been recovered and that two families in Gloucestershire have been informed. Talk to Dad; he will come by train on Monday. Phoned Nick to say what has happened and that I must stay longer. I hardly slept that night. A paralysing feeling of weight, fear and a pain in my heart. This is enormous. Shock brings you into the present like giving birth. All your energy goes into focusing on surviving. Some people die of it.

The parents of the "other student" who was one of the West victims, Therese Siegenthaler, died of grief before they knew what had happened to their beloved daughter.

Sunday 6th March

Decide to go to Gloucester police station. Spent two hours with John Bennett as he tried to explain the complexity of the case especially in relation to police competition with cheque book journalists.

We carried on South to break the news to two of my children who were boarding at a Quaker school. I was very anxious that they might find out by watching the six o'clock news. We had to get there before it broke. By the time we had arrived they had already found out by phoning their stepfather. It was hard to leave them there but we agreed that it would be the best solution for all of us. I also realised that their main concern was for my wellbeing. I have to find a way through that is positive but honest, for their sakes too. That has been one of the biggest challenges.

That night I lit a candle and prayed. I didn't watch the news.

My daughter has described her experience of this in a very moving piece that she wrote for the annual Dymond Speech Competition. It said a lot to me about her bravery and the caring atmosphere of the school. It nurtures pupils, helps them to explore quality in relationships and encourages them to question social and spiritual issues. The reality of Lucy's death has presented us all with huge questions about life and death.

Tuesday 8th March
Back in Wales. Went to have my hair cut. I wanted to have it shaved off as a gesture to the world that I was grieving, that something huge had happened and that I wasn't the same as I was before it happened. I am beginning to understand how ill-equipped we are as a society for coping with mourning. It would be helpful to bring back some external sign that someone is grieving. Black clothing has lost its significance since the Goths' fashion. While my hair was being cut (very short but not shaved) the news about Cromwell Street came on in the background. My hairdresser asked me what I thought about the awful goings on in Gloucester. I gulped and said something inane, thinking, "Does she really want to know?"

Friday 11th March
From the depth of suffering comes a release and a purification. The reality of Lucy's death rather than the imaginings of twenty years

brings a renewal of the preciousness of each moment of life. I must find the courage to go on and face the worst kind of death imaginable and somehow try to understand it.

*

For the past two years we have all been plunged into the powerful rapids of the thaw, each of us finding a way to stay afloat. However, under the turbulence was a wonderful surprise: a huge lake of warmth and compassion glowing, lapping, gently sustaining. It has been there throughout, sometimes in the material form of letters, phone calls, conversations, hugs. Sometimes it is less tangible but is to do with the best in humanity, the choice to send love in thoughts and prayers. Some of the communications were from people we hadn't heard from for twenty years. We felt so deeply grateful for that demonstration of support. It made a huge difference.

The closer I get to accepting Lucy's death the more I can remember about our childhood. Images come floating back. We grew up in a converted cider-mill in the middle of a Cotswold village. Our bedrooms were once storerooms for the apples, small with thick walls and tiny windows. Sometimes we would roast a few of the windfalls from the orchard on sticks, watching the juice spit in the flames and the skins bubble and blacken. Sometimes we would crush the apples in one of the cider presses, making the juice trickle around the stone groove, which was patterned with yellow lichens. This brew was known as Black Lady, and we would take it in turns to sip the sour gritty liquid, pretending it was a rare elixir. We often played games to do with getting around the "big room" without touching the ground. We had the freedom to explore the hill, making slides in the woods and swinging off creepers. We skidded around the "courtyard" on tricyles, veering onto two wheels around the sharpest corner past the lavender bush. There was a perfume of lavender and wallflowers in the summer and the sound of the pressure cooker hissing with soup or stew.

I remember a massacre of guinea pigs by a fox. Lucy carefully buried each mauled corpse. A close childhood friend told us about another incident with a dead guinea pig. "I was scared to kiss him as he was dead. Lucy was very angry with me. She told me fiercely that just because something dies it doesn't mean that you should stop loving it and that everyone deserves to be kissed before going to Heaven."

We had a raft made of oil cans and planks of wood from the farm, which provided endless entertainment on the pond—ranging from timeless contemplation of newts, lying on our fronts gazing into the still water, to rougher battles which usually ended up with someone falling in. I can still remember the smell of that muddy, weedy water.

In teenage years we spent less time doing things together.

Murder in the Dark and Postman's Knock with our cousins and local village friends were always popular games as we moved into adolescence. I was always off riding our pony. I remember that Lucy always seemed to be copying what I was doing (like learning the viola) which was irritating. Actually she was going her own way and writing sophisticated poetry. I was not kind to my younger sister at times. I don't feel guilty now, just sad that we didn't share more time together, express more love.

By the time that Lucy was twenty-one years old, we were both studying English at university (I'd had a few diversions on the way ... well, it was the late Sixties), both in our final year. I was in London and she was in Exeter. We enjoyed reading and discussing T.S.Eliot together because we loved the concept of "the still point of the turning world" in *Four Quartets*. We were fascinated by the exploration of the intersection of time with eternity. Lucy's focus was on truth and beauty. She was single-mindedly and passionately exploring the deeper meaning of life; immersed in art, literature and religion. Somehow she was untouched by the impact of the Sixties and yet very much in touch with deeper values, which she expressed in a way that was "indelible" (to use a word chosen by one of her friends). She was emerging into adulthood with a powerful inquiring mind and a sense of vision.

During her last free evening, 27th December 1973, Lucy visited a friend in Cheltenham. She left in time to catch the 10.15 bus back to Gretton. Her satchel contained my last present to her. It was a Victorian cut-glass jar, the right size to hold a night-light candle. It was the colour of amethyst, and could be hung on a Christmas tree or in a window by its wire handle, casting a soothing, pale-purple glow; resonant of sun light shining through stained glass in a place of worship—meditative; or maybe the colour of the air at dawn, just before the sun appears. Lucy had been delighted with it, and talked of using it as her nightlight when she was back in her hall of residence after the Christmas holiday.

Also in her bag was a book called *Pearl*. This medieval allegory is about the premature death of a pure maiden or young child and explores her father's grief and his journey towards consolation.

Finally, there was the letter of application to the Courtauld Institute of Art, for a postgraduate course in medieval art. It was never posted.

This is where, for me, it all goes into slow motion. The moment when Lucy, satchel swinging on her shoulder, hurried through the darkest of nights—there was a national power cut due to the fuel crisis—intending to post the letter before the bus came. The moment when Lucy's life met its opposite.

The gargoyles came to life and destroyed her.

Euphemisms serve to numb the senses and present the unpresentable. Maybe that is the best I can do. No, try again. I am avoiding it. Put it into words.

It is medieval Hell. It smacks of concentration camps and nuclear bombs.

I am trying to imagine the moment when she was abducted from her own direction in life and debased into a physical object to be treated as mere flesh and bones for the gratification of some other human beings whose quest was the opposite to hers. They stole her, gagged her, tied her up, toyed with her, raped her, tortured her, and at some unknown time, killed her.

They didn't know the beauty of her soul.

They caused her unimaginable physical and emotional suffering. How long was she kept alive, unable to scream or struggle? I pray that her recent conversion to Roman Catholicism gave her some moments of strength. They beheaded and dismembered her and stuffed her into a small hole, surrounded by leaking sewage pipes—head first, face down, still gagged. Her flesh decomposed into a tarry black slime that stained the clay walls of the hole and coated the bones. The rope that held her in bondage, two hair grips, a few strands of hair and the masking-tape gag survived, with most of her bones. Who knows what happened to the missing bones?

Did the Wests read the newspaper reports during the national search, and see her photograph stuck to trees and walls? We searched for her, desperately. We lost her for twenty years. How many people knew she was there but didn't say anything?

I am speaking from my heart about what we lost. Lucy had kindness, sensitivity, humour, warmth. The photograph that you see on the cover was taken in the summer of 1973 by my father during a visit to him in Yorkshire. We were at Fountains Abbey. It was the last time we spent together on our own. Lucy had me labelled as an incorrigible Romantic. The underlying implication was that I was a bit undisciplined and prone to Flights of Fancy And Imagination. I gently teased her for being a bit on the Classical side, preferring a Clear Structure and Lots Of Discipline. We talked a lot about our parents and tried to understand why they had got divorced. We were beginning to reform and deepen our relationship. I was the one who hitch-hiked everywhere, explored flower power and fashion, lived with my boyfriend. Lucy claimed to "do the opposite" of those around her. She was renowned for being "sensible". She protected her vulnerability with an acerbic wit and an ability to be witheringly critical. Her attitude towards me seemed to be a mixture of disapproval and admiration. I was beginning to appreciate her company and develop a great respect for her.

In a letter written to a friend, dated 1st June 1973, from Upton Pyne, Exeter, she wrote: "I think I have changed quite a lot in the last few months, not fundamentally, but in the way of a general softening up of sharp edges, and being more accepting." She spoke about her conversion to Roman Catholicism: "Although I still can't bear the idea of being a convert, I'm extremely happy about it and can't think why I didn't do something about it sooner."

In the same letter she spoke of one of her tutors. "One of his poems, which for some reason incorporates a lot of American Jazz idiom ends:

stick around, puss-cats
we're all in this together

and has almost become the motto of the medieval department. I frequently mutter it to myself as I bicycle dangerously along the New North Road." Later in the letter she refers to the "medieval group" which "has, from being such unpromising material, as I thought, turned into a very friendly company".

She wrote about the impending finals (which she never had the opportunity to take): "Just wait until the finals. Everyone will have forgotten about this year and no one will credit my predictions. It's sheer waste of time and crying in the wilderness to tell all these clever people that they're going to bluff their way through some more exams just like they have and always will do."

Talking more of the course, she said: "The most enjoyable literature studies have been the lyric and the romance, and almost all the art has been good. We went on a field trip to the Gloucester area for a weekend, and I was amazed how much we had absorbed, and could apply".

*

June 1994

The "remains" have not been released for burial. The careful plans for the funeral have been put on hold. So Lizzie (another close friend of Lucy), Chloe (my dear friend), my mother and I decided to go ahead with our memorial gathering to celebrate Lucy's life, even though we had intended it to be after the funeral. On a hot afternoon in July, 130 people gathered together at the Friends Meeting House in Cheltenham. My mother, in her introduction to Lucy's poems, said: "Members of our family, childhood friends, school friends, university friends and teachers spoke eloquently and beautifully about their memories of Lucy, touching on every facet of her complex character. She lived again for us and we all came away feeling truly uplifted".

Thank you, everyone for that display of love. It was truly inspiring and a great moment of healing for all of us. As my daughter Marigold reminded us in her speech, quoting from the Quaker Peace Testimony: "All the darkness in the world cannot put out the light of one candle".

A friend of mine who also became one of Lucy's friends said this about her: "She was like a flame and implacably true. There was no place in her life for convenient compromise. I think we should see her life as a life completed, short though it was, not as a life disrupted and cut off too soon. She had, in her way, reached a culminating point where her early life was complete, leaving her ready for something quite new. The gifts she brought with her and which she gave to us, as well as her example, will stay with us, and no one who knew her will ever forget her nor remain untouched by her."

The significance of the field trip to Gloucester that Lucy mentioned in her letter was not lost on those who attended the memorial gathering. One friend said:

"A few weeks ago my eye was caught by an article in one of the papers. It was a relation of the journey that the author had taken to a number of churches in the Hereford and Gloucestershire area, medieval churches, which he had seen on the visit. And it took me back on a journey that we had made twenty one years ago this summer, to see those very same churches—Kilpeck, Much Marcle—I'm sure you are familiar with this area. This was a field trip for the medieval group; we went around and looked at the churches and enjoyed the things that Lucy liked very much. Looking back on it now, it seemed very much a time of innocence. The sort of purity and innocence that has been mentioned before, today, was very much how it feels to me, looking back on it. It was much more related to the end of our childhood than to the beginning of adulthood and what went after it. I think, maybe for us Lucy's disappearance marked the first rumblings, if you like from the other world, or the underworld of uncertainty and suffering and loss and grief—and maybe even death—we had not encountered until then."

*

May 1994

The legal process that we were trapped in moved slowly, beyond our control. I arranged to go to Cardiff with two close friends to perform another ritual. It was time to rescue and protect, in some way, Lucy's physical remains. We went in the spirit of love with a need to make the experience more real and personal. We had waited twenty years to know where Lucy was and we still couldn't have a funeral. The investigation team at Gloucester kindly made the practical arrangements.

I would like to thank the dear man who allowed us to go beyond merely sitting in a chapel of rest next to a full sized coffin covered with a purple cloth fringed with gold tassels. I will never forget the look of understanding that came into his eyes when I emphasised that I wanted to place some special objects in with Lucy's bones. I know that some people might not understand my need to do this, but I have been pleasantly surprised by the number of people who did. It was a chance to love and cherish what was left of her. It was a chance to act in a situation that was still out of our hands. It was a chance to reclaim her from her murderers and the hugely disrespectful, wretched hole in the cellar of 25 Cromwell Street.

The mortician unscrewed the coffin to reveal two cardboard boxes. The larger of the two was exactly like the boxes I keep my A4 files in, pale grey do-it-yourself "archive system", about twelve inches deep, fifteen wide and twenty long. I felt a moment of panic. I pointed to the smaller of the two boxes, which was plain brown with a hinged lid, and asked,"Is her skull in there?" As he nodded and began to lift the lid, I was filled with the knowledge of what to do. A feeling of strength came over me.

As we drew nearer I gasped at the beauty of her skull. It was like burnished gold and it was something that was part of Lucy that had survived to tell the tale. At that moment I was full of the joy of finding something that had been a part of Lucy after all these years. Not a glimmer of fear, not a morbid thought entered the experience. I lifted her skull with great care and tenderness and kissed her brow. I marvelled at the sense of recognition in its curves and proportion. I wrapped it, as I have wrapped my babies, in her "soft brown blanket", her snuggler. I pressed her to my heart. Before I placed her skull back, I laid a branch of heather entwined with sheep's wool from the top of Plynlimon in the bottom of the box. I visualised the space and beauty of the wild mountain top on a summer's day: the brown peat, the sheep, the warm wind, the distant range of receding mountains, close to the sky. A place Lucy would have loved; a place that feels close to our Welsh roots; a place of freedom. I offered it with so much love.

When Lucy was eleven years old she gave me a little woven woollen bag. It says a lot to me about her qualities then. In order to make the bag she collected pieces of stray sheep's wool from the fences and hedges, probably from a field known as "the top ground" where we kept our pony. Then she made the carders to tease out the wool by breaking off individual thorns from rose bushes and pushing them through two rectangles of cardboard. Next she spun the wool with a spindle made from a pencil and a cotton reel. Finally she made a small loom and wove the spun wool into my much treasured bag. The whole process must have taken days of intense concentration, patience and a determination to follow an idea through in practice. It speaks of her gentleness and her generosity and her desire to get back to first principles. The bag is one of my most treasured possessions. I keep my embroidery threads in it.

Beryl, (one of Lucy's childhood friends), placed Chocka (a much loved, very worn soft toy lion stuffed with straw) and One-Eyed Bunny, dressed in his smart velvet trousers, to sit either side of her wrapped skull, tucking a posy of primroses under Bunny's arm. These toys had been involved in endless games with us all as we grew up. Now they had the important job of guarding this physical presence of Lucy until we could have her back for the funeral.

The mortician stood throughout this ceremony holding the lid of the larger box, nodding with approval. At one point he said "I wish more people could be doing this". When we had finally finished, he screwed down the lid of the coffin. We asked for some time to ourselves, turned the fluorescent light off, lit a candle, and stood in silence holding hands. I found myself thinking of every member of my family as if they were gathered there too. I was in another dimension, as if time had been transcended. Somehow we were united again within the "still point of the turning world". Something had been shifted. A step towards peace had been made.

For the rest of the time that Lucy's bones were still an "exhibit" for the defence I chuckled at the thought of the pathologist grumbling about interfering relatives, knowing that we had done the right thing. Through that experience I had the opportunity to transform the language from the crude butchery of the basement towards a poetry that we shared in our childhood. This was real and tangible evidence of her death.

Sometimes I return to the image of her skull as a way to release my grief. The orifices of the eye sockets remind me of the delicacy of her eyes that are no longer here, and never will be. They are empty holes, graves, the difference between being alive and being dead. The passing of time is reflected in the bones. The wonder at the durability of their substance and the beauty of their form increases my own sense of being alive. They remind me of my mortality and my physical structure. I feel deeply grateful for that unique, very intimate experience, an opportunity to pay tribute to Lucy in my own way, to begin to say goodbye, for real.

*

October 1994

Frederick West's solicitor insisted on keeping the "remains" as his "exhibits", despite the fact that they had been well documented by the police. The coroner wrote to him threatening to seek a judicial review of the situation.

12th December 1994

The coroner wrote to my parents again. "I have reluctantly to write to tell you and all other relatives and next of kin of the victims concerned in the Frederick West enquiry, to say that despite repeated attempts to reach agreement for the release of the remains, I have so far been unsuccessful ... Unfortunately I shall have to leave the matter over the Christmas period in view of the contentions put forward by those acting for Mr. West, but you may rest assured that I will reconsider the position early in the New Year and may well take further advice as to whether, notwithstanding the lack of agreement, in view of my duty to all the relatives and indeed, of course, to the public at large, grounds may exist for me to release the remains irrespective of the wishes of those defending Mr. West."

Twenty days later Frederick West solved this problem by killing himself.

6th February 1995

The committal trial for Rosemary West began. Carol, who has been my mother's friend since they were eight years old, attended it with me. It was very comforting to be able to share this torturous experience. We both felt the need to find out as much as we could about the reality of Lucy's death, before it became public knowledge. During my attendance at the trial I felt truly supported by the investigation team in a way that went beyond the job description. My only complaint was the dinners. (But not the puddings!).

I found it almost impossible to match the figure of Rosemary West, sitting in the dock , with the endless graphic details of sexual depravities and brutality that were read out hour after hour for five days by the barrister. He spoke with an impeccable Queen's English accent and no emotion. The rigid structure of the court proceedings had the effect of modifying the impact of the grotesque details of the case.

It was when I heard Rosemary Wests's voice on the tape-recorded police interviews with her about her relationship with her daughter Heather that I began to have some insight into her mind. I soon got the feeling that her deviant ignorance sprang from the fact that she had rarely known beauty, truth or love. I tried to imagine growing up in an environment where fear and abuse were the main components. Her most common epithet was predictable but disturbingly accurate in the context of her world: "bloody".

To her, education was a "bloody load of rubbish". And yet she managed to keep up appearances. About her children, she said, "I kept them clean, fit, walked them to school ... they never wanted for nothing." Heather "gave us a load of hassle when she grew up ... they just do what they likes". "When she left school she just sat in the chair" ... "Almost as if she didn't want to know me any more." "Once a child does cut you off, there is not a lot you can do."

Rosemary West's extreme frustration about Heather was crystallised for me when she said: "You can take a horse to water but you can't make him drink."

I began to get the picture of the power struggle that led to Heather's death (and that of Rosemary West's stepdaughter, Charmaine). I began to understand her need to have absolute control, to cause pain and ultimately death, that she acted out in the night life at 25 Cromwell Street: the deep violent rage of impotence and ignorance that led to such terrible cruelty; the impoverishment of a soul that knew no other way to live.

Her behaviour was bestial and brutal in its attempt to make her victims experience a feeling of extreme pain, humiliation and impotence. (All of which, one can presume, she was made to feel in some way during her own childhood?)

There was one little glimmer of insight into Rosemary West's imagination that both touched my heart and disturbed me. It was the only reference to beauty during a week full of endless statements of explicit, crude sexual detail, which were expanded upon in the recent trial. It was her attempt to lure Alison Chambers to come and live in Cromwell Street by promising her a life in the country at the weekends on "their farm" where she would be able "to ride horses and *write poetry*".

The image conjured up Lucy's world (Lucy spent a lot of her childhood involved in both activities). I began to sweat. Had Lucy had a chance to speak to them, or had they read about her life in the media shortly after they killed her, when we were desperately searching for her? Or was it simply unrelated, but one little moment when the world of the Wests brushed against Lucy's world on a more subtle level? That detail was used to lure another victim to their lair. There was something about the use of the word "poetry" that leapt out of the general mire of blasphemy and made my stomach churn.

Another such moment was when we heard that their last child was called Lucyanna ... a strange coincidence? Rosemary West was two years younger than Lucy.

*

14th February 1995

Nine months after our first visit to Cardiff and a week after the committal proceedings for Rosemary West, Beryl and I returned there. Frederick West's death meant that at last we were free to proceed with the funeral.

We had arranged to meet the undertaker from Exeter. She had been a student at Exeter University and was entirely supportive of any way that we chose to deal with what was a momentous occasion, charged with a huge need to express our love and our grief. Nick, my partner, had made a simple box for Lucy's bones. It looked like a medieval chest and was made from seasoned Welsh oak (kindly donated by another friend). The handles were made of thick rope. My boyfriend at the time of Lucy's "disappearance ", who now lives in Houston, Texas, sent a plaque of antique oak into which he had carved Lucy's name and dates:

LUCY KATHERINE PARTINGTON 1952-73

Nick had carefully mounted this with pegs on to the end of the box. This end became the "head end" for the purpose of carrying the coffin in and out of the church.

This time we had to go to the mortuary. The porter took a while to understand why we were there. He had to lock up at 4.00pm. It was already 2.45pm. The "file" box with its black felt tipped marking "JR5 Body 6" and in red felt-tip "Lucy Partington" awaited us on a trolley in the hall. This was my sister's last bureaucratic resting place. I had to reassure the porter that we had already seen the bones.

This society suffers badly from a fear of the reality of death. In Tibet, human thigh bones are lovingly made into exquisite-sounding instruments of great ceremonial importance.

Eventually the porter remembered that there was a chapel of rest next to the hall way. We were shown in, with the reminder that we had to be out by 4.00pm. The room had obviously been out of use for years. The mantlepiece was shrouded with dust. A blown egg that I had painted at Easter, with an image of a seal poking its nose out of the sea and a star fish sun, that I had placed carefully in the cup of the pelvis socket during our previous ritual, had been broken.

But it was time for the final re-ordering of the bones. We placed sawdust in the bottom of the box and then a length of Harris tweed that I had bought the previous autumn while exploring the wilderness of that island. We placed the skull at one end of the box and the pelvis at the other. Between these we laid the arm and leg bones. The vertebrae were threaded on a piece of rubber. We unthreaded them and laid them in order with the sacrum and coccyx next to the pelvis. The scapula, collarbone and ribs were arranged as symmetrically as possible in relation to the skull and the vertebrae. Handfuls of wrist, finger and toe bones and the patella were placed under the pelvis. I puzzled about the heel bone because it was quite small and looked as if it needed a socket with its ball-like end. Then I remembered Achilles' heel.

So, bones in order as much as is possible. Now to the gifts. First the book of Lucy's poems that my mother and stepfather had painstakingly collected together and published for family and friends. We proudly tucked a copy behind Lucy's skull after reading a few of the funny poems aloud, particularly one about Felix our pony. My father had sent a rosary blessed by the Pope. My younger son had sent the crucifix that he had bought from a nun during a holiday in France. My older son's offering was a piece of blue, shiny enamel work he had made. My daughter gave one of her intricate drawings of a Celtic knot. Nick gave a small jar of honey from our bees. Behind the pelvis I tucked a picture of the Dalai Lama. Chocka and Bunny and the " soft brown blanket" went in next. Finally Beryl laid one of her most beautiful weavings (a rich maroon Ikat scarf) over our treasure and we screwed down the lid. We carried the box out to the undertaker's car and she drove off to Exeter.

On 16th February 1995, seventeen days short of a year since we had found out what had become of Lucy, approximately twenty one years and seven weeks after her death, we could have the funeral.

The requiem mass hosted by Exeter University and conducted by Lucy's priest was full of the beauty and love that she deserved. Many of the friends and relatives who had attended the memorial gathering the previous July were there, also various friends who had been unable to go to that. Three of the investigation team sped down the M5 to be with us. It was particularly moving to see and hear the choir singing and the musicians playing. They were all present day students to whom Lucy was a sad but rich legend. I think we all experienced what Joseph Campbell once said: "Love is the pain of being truly alive".

The following day our family and a few close friends met at a tiny medieval church near our home. We were about to perform the penultimate ceremony. There had been much discussion within the family about whether to cremate or bury Lucy's bones. My youngest son voiced what became the general consensus: "Lucy has been buried in a horrible way for twenty years, I think we should bury her in a nice way now."

I felt very strongly that she should be laid in consecrated ground, that we should have a grave and that her bones were left in peace rather than being ground up (which is what would have happened to them if she had been cremated) and just scattered. It seems that it was the right decision because the grave has indeed become a place where we can go to remember and pay tribute to her, and to grieve. Having lost her for so long, there is some comfort in having finally laid her to rest and in knowing where her bones are buried.

Fortunately, there was room for a grave in the churchyard of a place that was very special to Lucy. It was a place that she used to retreat to when she wanted some time to herself, when she was younger. More recently she had been writing a thesis on the medieval wall paintings that still decorate the interior. The images that oppose each other on the two main walls of the nave are strangely disturbing, because one of them contains echoes of the violence surrounding her death and in the other there is a clear reminder of the strength of her faith. The violent image is of a hunting scene. A hare is cornered and the hounds are about to pounce. Since reading Lucy's unfinished thesis, I realise there are various interpretations for this (what does the hare represent?). My initial reaction was to see the hare as a vulnerable soul about to be pounced upon by the hounds. The hunter brings up the rear of the chase.

On the opposite wall stands a figure of St Christopher, at least eight feet tall, wading through the sea with Christ on his shoulder and a staff in his hand. Even though the church is of Anglican denomination the vicar was keen to help us fulfil our wishes for Lucy. The Roman Catholic priest kindly travelled from Exeter with the undertaker the day after the requiem mass and blessed the grave.

After a brief service my father, my two brothers and I carried Lucy's box out into the cold wind. It had been raining for at least three months and just at that moment a shaft of sunlight poured down from behind a cloud. The three priests stood in a line in their billowing white robes. Lucy's priest blessed the grave. The sun shone on and we lowered the box into the earth. As we all drew near to gaze into the grave, a bantam cockerel appeared from nowhere and nonchalantly got on with its scratching and pecking. During our childhood we kept bantams. Lucy used to paint them sometimes. There was something deeply reassuring about this moment. As if we had done all that we could to express our love for Lucy and there was a sort of reply going on ... a real blessing. The undertaker commented later that she had never experienced the length and quality of the silence that held us all in that moment.

8th October 1995

Eight months later. I felt very anxious about the trial because I knew how profoundly shocking the details of life in 25 Cromwell Street were. I was deeply concerned about the possibility of children watching the horrors on the news or reading them in the papers. I imagined creating a massive diversion, a national campaign to hang poems in trees in memory of all victims of violence. I wanted to create an opportunity for people to make a positive gesture in the midst of the onslaught of the West trial; to be able to focus on the tragedy of the deaths of the victims rather than on the murderers and their profound sickness.

The idea came from one of Lucy's favourite poems by Yevtushenko called "I Hung a Poem On a Branch". The last lines read:

If we have trouble on the way,
   we'll remember
      that somewhere,
         bathed in light,
a tree
   is waving
     a poem
   and smiling we'll say:
      "We have to go on".

When most of us were kissing pictures of the Beatles, Lucy was kissing a picture of Yevtushenko! I gave her the book of his poems for Christmas in 1967. She was studying Russian O-level at the time.

Unfortunately I simply didn't have the time and energy to put my campaign into practice. At that time, though, I was excited to discover Tibetan prayer flags. They hang like rows of bunting, bright-coloured rectangles of cloth printed with spiritual blessings. In an ancient ritual, they are renewed each year to signify hope, transformation and the spreading of compassion. As the year progresses, the wind disperses the energy of the words, which carry the power to pacify and heal everything they touch. A row now charts the wind outside my kitchen window. Filling and emptying, they flap and fray, tracing the invisible.

*

For the first few weeks of the trial I felt as if I was riding the storm quite well. I relied on DC Russell Williams, our personal policeman from the investigation team, for my information. I avoided any media reporting. I put my energy into my family and my work.

Over the last two years Russell has become "Russ". He has kept us informed of the progress of the case and has been there to answer any questions that we had. He always gave us advance warnings of media releases before they hit the headlines. Throughout the trial he phoned with regular reports from Winchester, so it was unnecessary to read the distortions in the press.

And then the Fred West tapes were played. Someone phoned to commiserate with me about a report by one broadsheet that printed the obscene words verbatim and added to the degradation by including a tabloid subheading. I hadn't been aware of the calumnies, but at that moment I was seized by the need to know what had been printed in all of the papers. Russ provided me with a large bundle.

Why was I so incensed by West's fantasies about Lucy and the way they were published? What he did to her was far worse. It was something to do with the crude level of language that was so far from the literary refinements that Lucy was immersed in. It brought out my rage at the inappropriateness of Lucy's death, which just did not seem fitting to her life. It made me aware of the vast gap I needed to cross in order to be able to comprehend and forgive.

It was as if anyone who heard them or read them became a victim of his pornographic delusions—the print seeped into the air, as insidious as nerve gas. They words poured out by the skip-full, vile gabblings, an endless rubble of lies. They revealed the completely egotistical, brutish mentality of a human being who was utterly devoid of any sense of truth about himself or anyone else. Not only had he performed these monstrous murders but he had then distorted the truth about them into further pollutions, extending his cruel trademark. It was truly blasphemous.

I had no choice but to crusade.

He said that Lucy was "just a girl I was knocking off" claiming that after three months of what was "purely sex, end of story" she had "come the loving racket and wanted to live with me". He made out that he was doing her a favour and that it all went wrong because she wanted more than he did. He said, "I grabbed her by the throat and then I drove back to Gloucester. I brought the van up over the pavement, then I knocked the engine and lights out and let him cruise down to the back." In his description, Lucy and the van were both subjected to a "knocking" of one sort or another. He didn't seem to discriminate between the objects of his brutality.

He lumped all his victims into the same category, just bodies that were soon deprived of any individual identity, as their voices were muted and their features were smothered under the masking-tape gags that lasted longer than the flesh they were glued to. During his garbled confessions we could see his total lack of connection with reality in his attempts to justify the killings, as if somehow they weren't really all that much to do with him—as if they were happening in spite of him, like some snuff movie going on in the background. The fantasies were as disarticulated as the bodies by the time he had finished with them. He said about one of the victims, "I strangled her or held my hands round her neck." (Meaning she sort of strangled herself because his hands happened to be held around her neck?) Was his repetitive, sadistic behaviour some sort of attempt to get in touch with a feeling of being alive?

I simply couldn't bear the thought that even one person might have believed his words.

We had been warned that the prosecution had chosen this tape, partly because it was easy to prove that West's explanation about why he had to kill Lucy was insane fantasy, because my mother's statement could account for the time that she was supposed to have been involved with him. It could be backed up by Exeter University and the priest who was preparing her for entering the Roman Catholic church in November 1973.

In fact, it was the defence that used the tape because it had a statement about West being the only person involved in the murders. So for three days it hung in the air, unchallenged. I became extremely agitated. Brian Leveson QC assured my father that he would make it very clear in his rebuttal that the tape was a cruel lie. However the press obviously found it less important to print the truth. It wasn't sensational enough.

My next chance was Leveson's summing up in which he focused even more strongly on just how obscene the fantasy was in relation to Lucy's life.

No, even though I had been in touch with the Press Association asking them to brief the journalists covering the West case to pick up on that point and print it, no words appeared.

The police suggested that we could make a statement after the trial if we still felt it was necessary. I decided to bring the subject up when I met Brian Leveson during the lunch hour at the judge's summing up in Winchester. I was fighting for the refinement of Lucy's whole being that is so clearly reflected in the carefully-chosen words of her poems. Russ gently reminded me that we were dealing with murder, not Lucy's life.

Fortunately Brian Leveson could understand my feelings, especially when I read him two of Lucy's poems. His last words to me were: "I'm off to speak to the press about a subject that is dear to your heart." Apparently he briefed each journalist individually and that evening the only news on radio and television put the jury's task into a nutshell, using Lucy as a focus. They had to decide between Fred West's version or Lucy's mother's statement. And why would Fred West have felt it necessary to create his story about Lucy if it wasn't to protect someone else (i.e. Rose)? The verdict reflected the truth.

*

19th March 1996

"Hello, Marian, it's Russ. Just to let you know that Rose West's leave for appeal has been turned down this afternoon, despite the fact that it was due to go on until the end of the week. As far as we're concerned, that's the end of the matter. If you want to give me a ring you can ... Thanks very much. Message ends."

It happened in an English city, in an ordinary terraced house, and it wasn't challenged for twenty years. It surpassed the limits of our understanding in its level of cruelty, going way beyond relentless abuse within the family. The Wests pushed sado-masochism to its logical conclusion and needed an influx of live human victims to feed their habit. In hindsight, the symptoms of their profound sickness festered in numerous eruptions. Apparently, life in 25 Cromwell Street didn't seem all that out of order, relatively speaking, so long a one didn't look too closely.

I have recently read these words of His Holiness the Dalai Lama:

I will learn to cherish beings of bad nature
And those pressed by strong sins and suffering
As if I had found a precious
Treasure very difficult to find

I know Lucy would have understood their meaning. "Love thine enemy". This path offers a way to break the cycle of violence and hatred, to find in danger the opportunity for change. To reach towards the experience of the deepest compassion (empathy with suffering) and humility (from the Latin word "humus", meaning ground or earth). The earth is common to all forms of life. It is that which connects us and feeds the following generations.

During the judge's summing up at Winchester I experienced a brief moment of this feeling of unconditional compassion. Anne Marie (Frederick West's daughter and Rosemary West's stepdaughter) was sitting behind me in the gallery, a few feet away. It was her gruelling evidence of continual sexual abuse by both parents that was being dealt with in this session. I felt profoundly sad for her. As we stood up to leave, I found myself reaching out my hand towards hers and saying something inadequate but heartfelt. We both had tears in our eyes. She moved her hand towards mine and touched it lightly. I'm not sure if she knew who I was.

I feel a great need to express my gratitude to Anne Marie, and to all those people who have given of their best during this deeply traumatic experience: family , friends, professionals, the jury and the witnesses. But I would especially like to thank the investigation team, who all showed great sensitivity and kindness.

I attended the judge's summing up at Winchester partly because it was the best opportunity to thank and hug (they are quite cuddly these policemen!) John Bennett, Terry Moore (who used to go on the same school bus as me) and dear Russ (I miss you already). "Good on you all" as we say in Gloucestershire.

Commitment to "Good" seems vital to our survival. It is a journey that each one of us needs to take. It involves looking at the darker side of our human nature as well as the lighter side. As human beings, the Wests have demonstrated how seriously individuals can go wrong. Our society has demonstrated how seriously we can all go wrong by not nurturing respect for ourselves and each other. It is time to speak out and learn from this tragedy, even though it is easier to ignore it or write it off as too weird to comprehend. Events like this hold a mirror up to our society. It is time to face our selves. Every one of us has this responsibility.

So, finally, let me take you on a journey, back to November 1973 when Lucy was received into the Roman Catholic Church. It was a big step to take, coming from an agnostic background (although our great-grand parents were missionaries in China). Her faith was fresh and real. Five weeks later she suffered a death that went way beyond our worst imaginings. The priest who received her into the church assures me that even though she was murdered, she would have died in a state of grace (a divine, strengthening influence). Fortunately he was able to perform her requiem mass, twenty one years after her death. Later on, I asked the dear priest if he thought that Lucy's faith would have helped her in her terrifying ordeal, one of those unanswerable questions in the league of "Why did it happen to Lucy?" Was it really as random as "She was in the wrong place at the wrong time"? (We have to learn to live with all this. We have to accept that it really did happen.) However, he meditated quietly for a while and said, "Well, it's just a feeling that I've got, but I do feel that she would have maintained her integrity." Knowing Lucy's intellectual and spiritual refinement, I can mostly believe that. I pray that her faith gave her strength.

Lucy's suffering ended twenty two years ago, when ours began. Four months after her disappearance I had a dream. Lucy came back and I asked her where she had been. She said, "I've been sitting in a water meadow near Grantham, and *if you sit very still you can hear the sun move*." This image filled me with a profound feeling of peace, the kind that "passeth understanding". I woke up with this feeling. It lasted for a few seconds. I've never forgotten it.

Thank you Lucy. Your life and your death have deepened my knowledge of love. I will try to pass that on. Each moment that passes is full of significance and the opportunity for change, if we choose to look, if we choose to act.

Maybe we could start with each one of us writing a favourite poem on a small piece of cloth and tying it to the branch of a tree, in memory of all victims of violence and as an act towards hope for a world in which cruelty is replaced by understanding and compassion.

It is time to salvage the sacred.

*